I0901687

# A Trip Through the BIBLE

written by Tracy Harrast
illustrated by Richard Johnson

KREGEL Kidzone

# God's Great Creation

**Genesis 1–3**

In the beginning, God looked over the darkness and said, "Let there be light," and there was light. This was the world's first day. On the second day, God spread a sky out over the waters. The third day was when He separated land from ocean and covered the land with plants. Each day, He saw that it was good.

Next, on the fourth day, God made the sun and moon. Then He made birds and fish on the fifth day. On the sixth day, God created the rest of the animals and then the first man and woman, Adam and Eve. He made the people in His own image, His own likeness, and He gave them a beautiful garden named Eden where they could live. He put Adam and Eve in charge of all of the animals. God told them they could eat from any tree in the garden except the tree of the knowledge of good and evil. He warned that if they ate from that tree, they would die.

**On the first day, God created light.**

**On the second day, God created the sky.**

Did you know?

God gave Adam the very important job of naming every animal in the garden!

**On the fourth day, God created the sun, moon, and stars.**

**On the third day, God created the land, sea, and every kind of plant.**

> **Did you know?**
> God created Eve from Adam's rib because God said it was not good for the man to be alone.

**On the fifth day, God created the creatures of the sea and sky.**

One day, a serpent lied to Eve. He said she would not die if she ate the forbidden fruit. Eve believed him and thought the fruit looked delicious, so she ate some. Then she gave some to Adam, and he ate too. Immediately, they knew they had done wrong and hid from God. Before their sin, they could have lived forever in the garden. Now they had to leave the garden and would one day die just as God had warned. God made clothes of animal skins for them to wear out of the garden.

# Noah and the Flood

**Genesis 6:5–9:17**

People on Earth eventually turned from God and became so evil that God decided to flood the world to wipe them out. Noah had remained faithful to God, and he obeyed when God told him to build an ark. The cypress wood ark was 450 feet long with three levels and one door. When Noah and his sons—Ham, Shem, and Japheth—finished the ark, God sent animals.

Pairs of every kind of animal boarded the ark. There were seven of every kind of "clean" animal (ones that could be eaten) and every kind of bird. Then Noah, his wife, their three sons, and their sons' wives climbed aboard, too. After the Lord shut the door, the storms began. Rain fell for 40 days and nights. Everyone who was not on the ark drowned.

Did you know?

The ark was longer than twelve school buses lined up end to end!

**Noah didn't have to catch the animals. God sent the animals to the ark.**

After forty days, the rain finally stopped, and gradually the water went down. The ark came to rest on the top of Mount Ararat. Noah opened a window and sent out a raven and later a dove. The raven and dove could not find a place to rest, so each returned. Seven days later, Noah sent the dove out again. It returned with an olive leaf, so Noah knew some land was dry. Noah sent the dove out again seven days later, and it did not return. Noah released all of the animals and then built an altar to worship the Lord.

**The rain fell for forty days and forty nights. Even the highest mountain was covered with twenty feet of water.**

Did you know?

The Earth was covered with water for 150 days before the ark rested on Mount Ararat.

**God created a rainbow as a reminder of His covenant—His promise to people to never completely flood the world again.**

# Joseph Forgives

**Genesis 37, 39–45:5**

Jacob had 12 sons, but Joseph was his favorite. Jacob gave Joseph a fancy coat, which made Joseph's brothers furious. God gave Joseph a gift, too—Joseph could figure out the meaning of dreams. One day, Joseph explained that he had had two dreams. They both meant someday his brothers would bow to him. When they heard this, Joseph's brothers hated him even more. They decided to throw Joseph into a pit and kill him. Later, they changed their plan and sold Joseph to merchants who took Joseph to Egypt. The brothers gave his torn, bloody coat to their father to make him think a wild animal had eaten Joseph. A man named Potiphar bought him from the merchants.

### Did you know?

Joseph dreamed that his brothers were sheaves (bundles) of wheat bowing to his sheaf of wheat. He also dreamed that his parents were the moon and sun, and his brothers were stars, all bowing down to him.

**Jacob gave Joseph a beautiful coat, but he didn't give one to any of his other sons.**

**Joseph's brothers dipped his coat in goat's blood to trick Jacob.**

Potiphar's wife falsely accused Joseph of a crime, and he was sent to prison. Joseph became the leader of the prisoners, and God helped him tell the prisoners what their dreams meant. When Pharaoh needed to know the meaning of his dream about seven skinny cows that ate seven fat cows, Joseph was brought to him. Joseph explained that Egypt would have seven years when food would grow, followed by seven when it would not. Pharaoh freed Joseph and put him in charge of storing food for the coming famine.

**Joseph interpreted Pharaoh's dreams of seven fat cows and seven skinny cows.**

Joseph was the most powerful leader in Egypt other than Pharaoh. When Joseph's brothers were starving, they came to Egypt to beg for food and bowed to Joseph just as they had in his dream. They didn't recognize Joseph, but he recognized them! As cruel as they had been to him, he forgave them anyway. He saw that God had brought good out of what they had done—because Joseph had become a leader, God had saved many lives through him.

### Did you know?

Benjamin was Joseph's only "true" brother (Rachel was their mother). His other ten brothers had a different mother (Leah).

# Moses Frees the Slaves

**Exodus 2–20:17**

The pharaoh of Egypt used God's people, the Israelites, as slaves for many years. To save her baby son, an Israelite woman put him in a basket and placed him at the river's edge. Pharaoh's daughter found the baby and named him Moses. She raised him as her own child.

Moses left Egypt when he was grown and became a shepherd in Midian. He was tending sheep one day when he heard God speak from a flaming bush that did not burn. God had heard the millions of Israelite slaves praying for freedom. He decided to send Moses to lead them out of Egypt. Moses thought he could not lead because he could not speak well, but people do not have to be perfect to serve God.

## Did you know?

God fed the Israelites manna when they were in the desert. Manna was bread that appeared on the ground like dew every morning.

**Plagues of Egypt**

**All water became blood • frogs • gnats • flies • dead livestock • boils • hail • locusts • three days of darkness • death of firstborn sons**

Moses went to Pharaoh and told him to let God's people go. When Pharaoh wouldn't free them, God sent ten terrible events called plagues to persuade Pharaoh to let the Israelites leave. When all the firstborn sons in Egypt died, including Pharaoh's own son, Pharaoh ordered the Israelites to leave Egypt. Pharaoh changed his mind, though, and chased them with his army of chariots. God parted the Red Sea so Moses and the Israelites could escape on dry land, and then closed the water over the Egyptian army. God's people were free.

In the wilderness, the Israelites were rebellious and did not want to go where God said, so He let them wander. During their journey, God wrote ten rules on stone tablets for Moses to give the people. These are the Ten Commandments. Forty years after leaving Egypt, God's people entered Canaan, the Promised Land.

**Israelite slaves in Egypt were abused and forced to make bricks. When they cried out to God, He heard them and sent Moses to free them.**

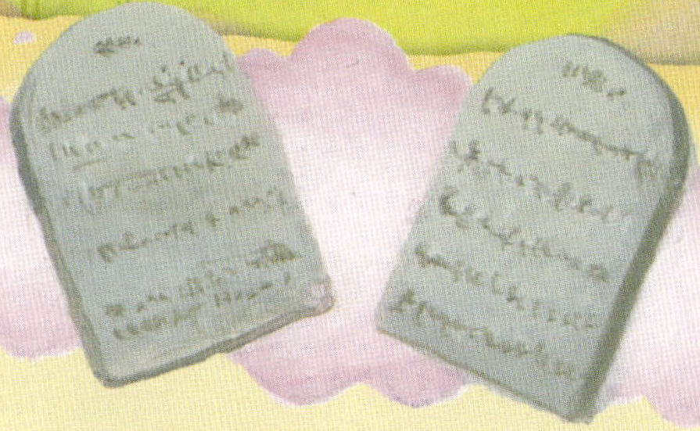

**The Ten Commandments**

1. Do not have any other gods.
2. Do not make any idols.
3. Do not misuse the Lord's name.
4. Keep the Sabbath day holy.
5. Honor your father and mother and you will have a long life.
6. Do not murder.
7. Do not commit adultery.
8. Do not steal.
9. Do not lie.
10. Do not covet.

## Did you know?

God was with the Israelites as they traveled through the desert. He appeared as a pillar of cloud during the day and a pillar of fire during the night.

# David and the Giant

**1 Samuel 16–17:50**

David was a shepherd boy who played his harp for King Saul. The king liked David so much that he made David one of his armor-bearers. One day when David brought food to his brothers during a battle, a giant Philistine named Goliath stood between the armies. Goliath shouted that if one man fought him and won, that man's army would win. If that man lost, Goliath's army, the Philistines, would win.

Everyone in Saul's army was too afraid to fight Goliath. But David wasn't afraid, and he told Saul that he would defeat the giant. David remembered that God was with him when he had saved his father's sheep from a lion and a bear. He told Saul that God would save him from the giant. David placed a stone in his sling, swung it around, and let the stone fly. When it sank into Goliath's forehead, the giant fell on his face. David had won the battle!

**Did you know?**

David had only five stones in his pouch. He had gathered them from a nearby stream.

**King Saul lent David his armor. It was too big, so David fought without any armor.**

**Did you know?**

David wrote many songs praising God. These songs are in the Bible in a book called Psalms.

**Goliath stood more than nine feet tall!**

# Jonah's Lesson

**Jonah 1–4**

God saw that the city of Nineveh had become evil, so He told a man named Jonah to travel to that city to preach. Jonah didn't want to go and he tried to run from God. He got on a boat that was sailing toward Tarshish instead. God sent a huge storm that almost sank the boat. Jonah knew that the storm was his fault. He told the other terrified sailors the storm would stop if they tossed him into the sea, so they did.

God sent a great fish to rescue Jonah from drowning. The fish swallowed Jonah, and he stayed in the fish's belly for three days and three nights. Finally when Jonah promised to obey God, the fish spat Jonah onto the sand. Jonah went to Nineveh to preach, and the people listened to him and repented.

**Did you know?**

Jesus told His disciples He would be in the tomb the same number of days that Jonah was in the great fish.

**During the storm, frightened sailors tossed everything they could overboard...including Jonah!**

# God's Son Is Born

Matthew 1:18–25, 2:11; Luke 1:26–38, 2:1–20

One day an angel named Gabriel appeared to a young woman named Mary. He told her that God was pleased with her and that she would give birth to the Son of God. Mary was confused. But Gabriel said, "With God nothing is impossible." Mary loved God and agreed to do whatever He asked. Gabriel also appeared in a dream to Joseph, the man Mary was to marry, and said, "Do not be afraid to take Mary as your wife. The baby inside her is from the Holy Spirit. You should name Him Jesus, for He will save His people from their sins."

When Mary was about to have the baby, she and Joseph traveled to Bethlehem to be taxed. The inn was full, so Mary and Joseph stayed in a stable nearby. After Jesus was born, Mary wrapped Him in strips of cloth and laid Him in a manger.

That night shepherds were watching their sheep when an angel appeared and said, "I bring you good news of joy for all people. Today your Savior, Christ the Lord, was born! You will find Him wrapped in strips of cloth and lying in a manger." Suddenly the sky was full of angels praising God.

The shepherds hurried to Bethlehem to see the baby, and they praised God. Later, wise men followed a star until it led them to a house where Jesus was with His mother. The wise men worshipped Him and gave Him gifts of gold, frankincense, and myrrh.

### Did you know?

Mary and Joseph were "espoused," which was like being engaged. They had been through a ceremony in which they had made formal promises to marry, but they were not married yet when Gabriel visited Mary.

**Jesus was born in a humble stable with a manger for His crib. A manger is an animals' feed box.**

### Did you know?

We assume there were three wise men because the Bible mentions three gifts, but there could have been fewer wise men, or more.

# Jesus Works Miracles

**Feeding 5,000: Matthew 14:15–21, Mark 6:35–44, Luke 9:12–17, John 6:5–14**
**Walking on Water: Matthew 14:22–33, Mark 6:45–52, John 6:16–21**
**Blind Man at Bethsaida: Mark 8:22–25; Raising Lazarus: John 11:1–45**

A miracle is when God does what seems impossible. Jesus worked miracles throughout His three years of ministry that helped people realize that He was more than just a teacher—He was the Son of God. His first miracle was turning water into wine at a wedding. More than once He fed thousands. He calmed the sea during a storm and walked on the water. Jesus told Peter to pay his tax with a coin from a fish's mouth. Jesus healed people who couldn't see, hear, walk, or talk. He raised a twelve-year-old girl, a widow's son, and His friend Lazarus from the dead! Jesus even rose from the dead Himself.

**Did you know?**
After Jesus fed more than 5,000 hungry people, there were enough leftovers to fill twelve baskets!

When Jesus taught a crowd of more than 5,000 and they grew hungry, a boy shared his five loaves of barley bread and two small fish. That seemed like too little to feed so many. Jesus gave thanks to God, broke the bread and fish into pieces, and then there was enough to feed everyone!

One night the disciples took their boat across a lake, but Jesus stayed behind to pray. Later His disciples were amazed when Jesus caught up with them by walking on top of the water! Jesus even helped Peter walk on the water briefly. But Peter took his eyes off of Jesus, grew afraid, and began to sink. Jesus reached out and caught him.

To heal a blind man outside Bethsaida, Jesus spit on the man's eyes, put His hands on the man, and asked, "Do you see anything?"

The man answered, "I see people; they look like trees walking." Jesus touched the man's eyes again. Then the man could see clearly.

Jesus' friend Lazarus died and was buried in a tomb. When Jesus arrived four days later, He prayed and then called loudly, "Lazarus, come out!" Lazarus walked out of the tomb alive!

# Jesus Tells Parables

**Lost Sheep: Matthew 18:12–14, Luke 15:3–7; Good Shepherd: John 10:11–15; Wise and Foolish Builders: Matthew 7:24–27; Mustard Seed: Matthew 13:31–32, Mark 4:30–32, Luke 13:18–19; Good Samaritan: Luke 10:30–37**

Jesus told many simple stories called parables to help teach spiritual lessons. He told them to His disciples and to large groups of people. Parables make it easier to understand God's instructions.

In one parable, a shepherd had 100 sheep. One day, he noticed that one was missing. He left the flock and searched until he found the lost one. He was so happy when he found it that he carried it home on his shoulders and celebrated! He said everyone in heaven celebrates like that when only one person who has wandered from God returns to Him.

Jesus said people who hear His words and do what He says are like the wise man who built his house on a rock. When storms came, that builder's house stood firm. Jesus said whoever hears Him but does not do what He says is like the foolish man who built his house on sand. When storms came, that man's house fell with a crash. When problems come, a life built on obeying Jesus won't fall apart.

In Jesus' parable of the mustard seed, the tiniest seed grew so large that birds could perch in its branches. At first Jesus' kingdom was small with only a few believers, but now there are millions who follow Jesus.

Did you know?

Jesus said, "I am the good shepherd; I know my sheep and my sheep know me." A shepherd used his staff to free sheep when they got entangled in bushes or fell into danger.

**Jesus told parables about everyday life that helped people understand truth.**

Jesus told a parable about a traveler who was robbed and beaten. Two men saw the traveler and passed by without helping him—one was even a holy man. Then a man from Samaria—a hated foreigner—came by. The Samaritan stopped to care for the injured man even though their countries were enemies. The Samaritan cleaned and bandaged the traveler's wounds and even paid for the man to stay at an inn until he was well. Jesus said to love others as that good Samaritan did.

# Jesus' Last Week

**Matthew 21–26; Mark 11–14; Luke 19:28–22:62; John 12:12–19**

Jesus' last week before His death is now called Passion Week. On Sunday Jesus rode like a king into Jerusalem on the back of a donkey. People waved palm branches and shouted, "Hosanna!" which meant, "Save us!" When He visited the temple, Jesus saw that dishonest people were buying and selling. He became angry and threw them out of His Father's house.

During the week, Jesus told many parables and taught the greatest commandment: "Love God with all your heart, soul, and mind." He said the second greatest commandment is like it: "Love your neighbor as yourself." Meanwhile, jealous leaders plotted to kill Jesus and paid Judas, one of the disciples, thirty pieces of silver to tell them where they could capture Jesus.

**Today, we celebrate Jesus' ride into Jerusalem on a holiday called Palm Sunday.**

Did you know?

The donkey colt Jesus rode into Jerusalem had never been ridden before.

Jesus and His followers entered Jerusalem through one of the twelve gates that surrounded the city.

On Thursday Jesus and His disciples ate the Passover meal, Jesus' last supper. Jesus gave them pieces of bread to remind them of His body that would be broken for them. He gave them wine to remind them of His blood that would be poured out for sin. He promised to prepare a place in heaven for those who believe in Him.

Did you know?

An angel appeared to Jesus in the Garden of Gethsemane to bring Him strength.

Then Jesus went to the Garden of Gethsemane to pray for strength to do God's will, which would mean giving His life the next day. Judas showed up with guards and gave Jesus a kiss to identify Him. The guards arrested Jesus and took Him away.

# Jesus Lives

Matthew 27:11–28:10; Mark 15:1–16:6; Luke 23–24; John 18:28–20:30

Jesus was brought before the Roman governor Pilate, who couldn't find any reason to punish Jesus. The crowd demanded He be crucified and Pilate sent Jesus to Golgotha, where He was nailed to a cross between two thieves. Jesus cried, "It is finished," and died. The sky grew dark and an earthquake shook the ground.

After Jesus died, friends placed His body in a tomb. Guards rolled a heavy round stone in front of the tomb's entrance and sealed it. Jesus' body remained there until the third day when He rose from the dead. On that day, women brought spices to put on Jesus' body and found that an angel had rolled away the stone. The angel said to them, "He is not here; He has risen, just as He said He would." This was the first Easter.

**Jesus had to carry His own cross to Golgotha. Golgotha means "the place of the skull."**

**Did you know?**

After Jesus rose from the dead, He appeared to more than 500 people before returning to heaven.

**Jesus said, "God loved the world so much that He gave His only Son so that whoever believed in Him would live with Him forever."**

# Questions

Answers are on page 23.

1. What was the first thing God created?
2. Where in the Bible can you find the songs David wrote?
3. Jesus told stories to teach lessons. What were the stories called?
4. Which holiday celebrates the day Jesus rose from the dead?
5. What were the names of Noah's three sons?
6. Who found baby Moses in a basket?
7. What was the name of the angel who appeared to Mary?
8. What did bread represent at Jesus' last supper?
9. What were Jesus' last words when He was on the cross?
10. After telling the parable of the lost sheep, Jesus called Himself the good what?
11. Bread appeared on the ground like dew every morning for the Israelites. What was it called?
12. What was the first animal Noah released to find land?
13. What did Jesus say is the greatest commandment?
14. What was the name of the city where Jesus was born?
15. How long was Jonah inside the great fish?
16. What gift did Jacob give to his favorite son, Joseph?
17. How tall was Goliath?
18. In the lost sheep parable, how many sheep did the shepherd have before any strayed?
19. What is a covenant?
20. On what kind of animal did Jesus ride into Jerusalem on Palm Sunday?
21. In the parable of the good Samaritan, the Samaritan paid for the hurt man to stay where?
22. How many stones did David put in his pouch?
23. What part of Adam did God use when He made Eve?
24. Was Joseph Jesus' father?
25. Did God create plants before or after animals?
26. Where did the merchants take Joseph after his brothers sold him?
27. On the night of Jesus' birth, who saw the sky filled with angels praising God?
28. What reward did jealous leaders give Judas to betray Jesus?
29. How long was Jesus' body in the tomb?
30. According to Jesus' parable, what kind of seed was the smallest?
31. What stopped Jonah's ship from sailing to Tarshish?
32. How long did the Israelites wander in the wilderness after leaving Egypt?
33. What does "Hosanna" mean?
34. Which tree in the Garden of Eden had forbidden fruit?
35. Gabriel told Joseph that Jesus would save people from what?
36. How far above the highest mountain did the water rise from the great flood?
37. What ability did God give Joseph that helped Pharaoh?
38. The kind man who helped a crime victim in Jesus' parable was from which country?
39. Which three Egyptian plagues involved insects?
40. What sign did Judas give the guards to let them identify Jesus?
41. Before Jesus was born, why did Mary and Joseph have to go to Bethlehem?
42. Where did the guards arrest Jesus?
43. The rainbow reminds God and people of what?
44. Which man bought Joseph from the merchants?
45. In Pharaoh's dream, what did the fat cows represent?
46. After Jesus died on the cross, the sky got dark. What else happened?
47. What flaw did Moses think would keep him from being a leader?

48. How many people boarded the ark altogether?

49. What did God warn would happen if Adam and Eve ate the forbidden fruit?

50. How was the giant stone removed from Jesus' tomb?

51. What is a manger?

52. How did Jonah escape from the great fish?

53. What is the name of the place where Jesus was crucified?

54. During the first plague, what did every drop of water in Egypt become?

55. When the dove returned to Noah, what was in its beak?

56. Why did Mary have to give birth in a stable?

57. How did Joseph's brothers make their father think Joseph was dead?

58. In what kind of building did the wise men find Mary and Jesus?

59. According to the parable of the lost sheep, what happens in heaven when someone returns to God?

60. Did God create birds before or after people?

61. What was the name of the Promised Land?

62. What job did Pharaoh give Joseph when Pharaoh freed him from jail?

63. David trusted God because God had saved him from what two animals in the past?

64. What did wine represent at Jesus' last supper?

65. How did the good Samaritan's country and the hurt man's country feel about each other?

66. Where did David's rock hit Goliath?

67. Which two kinds of animals came on the ark in sevens instead of pairs?

68. In one of Pharaoh's dreams, what did the skinny cows represent?

69. What three gifts did the wise men bring Jesus?

70. In two different dreams, Joseph's brothers bowed to him. What did they look like in each?

71. Why did Eve eat the forbidden fruit?

72. What was unique about the flaming bush from which God spoke to Moses?

73. What blessing is attached to the commandment to honor your parents?

74. What did Jesus say is the second greatest commandment?

75. What was the name of the Roman governor that sent Jesus to be crucified?

76. Which of God's creations resemble Him?

77. Why did Jonah decide to sail to Tarshish instead of Nineveh?

78. On what day of the week did Jesus ride a donkey into Jerusalem like a king?

79. Why did God need to part the Red Sea for the Israelites?

80. How long did the rain fall while Noah was on the ark?

81. What did God make for Adam and Eve before they left the garden?

82. What were women bringing to Jesus' tomb on the first Easter Sunday?

83. How did the wise men know where to find Jesus?

84. What instrument did David play for King Saul?

85. What did the tiny mustard seed represent in Jesus' parable?

86. How did Jonah get in the water during the storm?

87. Who shut the door to the ark once the animals were on board?

88. Who did Jesus throw out of the temple in Jerusalem?

89. Why didn't David wear the armor King Saul lent to him to fight Goliath?

90. In the parable of the wise and foolish builders, people who hear Jesus' words and don't listen are like whom?

91. How many brothers did Joseph have?

92. Why did God make Eve?

93. What kind of wood did Noah use to build the ark?

94. What job did God give Adam in the Garden of Eden?

95. Gabriel appeared to Mary with good news, but he also appeared to someone else. Who?

96. Name three of the ten commandments.

# Answers

1. Light
2. Psalms
3. Parables
4. Easter
5. Ham, Shem, Japheth
6. Pharaoh's daughter
7. Gabriel
8. Jesus' body
9. "It is finished."
10. Shepherd
11. Manna
12. A raven
13. Love God with all your heart, soul, and mind.
14. Bethlehem
15. Three days and three nights
16. A colorful coat
17. More than nine feet tall
18. One hundred
19. A promise between man and God
20. Donkey colt
21. At an inn
22. Five
23. His rib
24. No, Jesus is the Son of God
25. Before
26. Egypt
27. Shepherds
28. Thirty pieces of silver
29. Three days
30. The mustard seed
31. A storm God sent
32. Forty years
33. Save us!
34. The tree of the knowledge of good and evil
35. Their sins
36. Twenty feet
37. Interpreting dreams
38. Samaria
39. Gnats, flies, and locusts
40. Judas kissed Jesus
41. To be taxed
42. The Garden of Gethsemane
43. God promised never to flood the whole world again.
44. Potiphar
45. Seven years when food would grow
46. There was an earthquake.
47. He could not speak well.
48. Eight
49. They would die.
50. An angel moved it.
51. An animal's feed box
52. It spat him onto the sand.
53. Golgotha
54. Blood
55. An olive leaf
56. There was no room in the inn.
57. They dipped Joseph's coat in blood.
58. A house
59. Everyone in heaven celebrates!
60. Before
61. Canaan
62. Storing the food
63. A lion and a bear
64. Jesus' blood
65. They were enemies.
66. On his forehead
67. Birds and "clean" (edible) animals
68. Seven years of famine when food would not grow
69. Gold, frankincense, and myrrh
70. Wheat sheaves and stars
71. She believed the serpent and the fruit looked delicious.
72. It was on fire, but did not burn.
73. You will live a long life.
74. Love your neighbor as yourself.
75. Pilate
76. People
77. He tried to run from God; he didn't want to preach to Nineveh.
78. Sunday
79. So they could escape from the Egyptian army that was chasing them
80. Forty days and forty nights
81. Clothes made of animal skins
82. Spices
83. They followed a star.
84. The harp
85. Jesus' kingdom
86. He asked sailors to throw him overboard.
87. God
88. Dishonest people who were buying and selling
89. It was too big.
90. The foolish man who built his house on the sand
91. Eleven
92. It was not good for the man to be alone.
93. Cypress wood
94. Naming the animals
95. Joseph
96. 
    1. Do not have any other gods.
    2. Do not make any idols.
    3. Do not misuse the Lord's name.
    4. Keep the Sabbath day holy.
    5. Honor your father and mother.
    6. Do not murder.
    7. Do not commit adultery.
    8. Do not steal.
    9. Do not lie.
    10. Do not covet.

Published by Kregel Kidzone,
an imprint of Kregel Publications
P.O. Box 2607, Grand Rapids. MI 49501
© 2011 Reader's Digest Children's Publishing, Inc.
Illustrations © 2009 Richard Johnson
All rights reserved. Reader's Digest and Reader's Digest Children's Books
are registered trademarks of The Reader's Digest Association, Inc.
Manufactured in China.
Conforms to ASTM F963
10 9 8 7 6 5 4 3 2 1
LPP/08/11